IN PRAISE
OF FOOTBALL

GABRIEL FITZMAURICE

IN PRAISE
OF FOOTBALL

Foreword by Tom Humphries

MERCIER PRESS
IRISH PUBLISHER – IRISH STORY

MERCIER PRESS
Cork
www.mercierpress.ie

Trade enquiries to CMD BookSource,
55a Spruce Avenue, Stillorgan Industrial Park,
Blackrock, County Dublin

© Gabriel Fitzmaurice, 2009

Introduction © Tom Humphries, 2009

ISBN: 978 1 85635 640 4

10 9 8 7 6 5 4 3 2 1

A CIP record for this title is available from the British Library

Printed and bound in the EU.

Mercier Press receives
financial assistance from
the Arts Council/An
Chomhairle Ealaíon

For Brendan Kennelly
Poet, Footballer, Kerryman

Sport has always been the material of epic, from Homer to Virgil and onwards. There is no sense that it is a lower subject for art than any other. Gabriel Fitzmaurice sees this better than anyone else currently writing in Ireland, writing of the heroes on the field from Con Brosnan to the great Mick O'Connell, but expressing too the generous fervour of the true supporter. This is a book in praise of Kerry and Moyvane, and it is right to salute the great local heroes. But it recognises too greatness and tragedy from Offaly or Tyrone, even extending post-Ban to the supporters of Munster and Leicester rugby. This is a broad-minded book that makes your heart beat faster in the same way that the sporting *gaisce* itself does.

Bernard O'Donoghue

Gabriel's poems will strike a chord (or maybe a keyboard!) with anyone who has been involved in sport at any level. There is a poignant nostalgia, for it all evokes memories of growing up through the various stages of sporting development. The references are brilliant throughout:

'his hero turns and, smiling, signs his name'
'nothing is, but is revealed and tested on the football field'
'it's losers who remember what went on'
'if he was a small bit faster, he'd be a poor man today'

The poems reveal an insight into a 'field' I did not think Gabriel could venture into so successfully. He has done this magnificently.

Eoin Hand

Another unique and superb publication from Gabriel. The beauty and enduring mysteries of football captured in verse for posterity in that beautiful Fitzmaurice style. His deep and passionate love for Kerry and sport in general comes shining through. A priceless collection.

Weeshie Fogarty

Gabriel Fitzmaurice understands better than most that football is a passionate and rugged expression of a people's soul. These poems speak of heroes, of tribes and of immortality. They sing of great deeds, of glory and of grace. Fitzmaurice's parishes and people are defined by the games and by how those games are played. Triumph, trophies, truth and betrayal are 'things insufficient till they're sung'. His song is worth listening to.

Dara Ó Cinnéide

Fitzmaurice goes back to the village and the province he came from for universality; whether it be a conversation in a pub between former greats elevating myth to legend, or an ode to a Mikey or a Bomber or Galliamh, his poems hit the inward eye. Pictures evolve from the printed page and you are there when the glorious deeds are performed. Gabriel Fitzmaurice togs out and holds his own with our finest poets. His every kick finds its target unerringly. Fitzmaurice never drops a pass. There is no better way to honour our sporting heroes.

Billy Keane

Thanks for your football poems. I found them very interesting and to the point, very much. Memories of times gone by with the mention of Con Brosnan, John Joe Sheehy, Mícheál O'Hehir, we met them all. A couple of lines from *At the Ball Game* hit the nail on the head dead on:

> 'No cup, no trophy will redeem
> Victory by ignoble means.'

Should be the first lesson to anyone who aspires to the name of 'sportsman'. Alas ...

Mick O'Connell

What struck me most was not just the obvious, i.e. the celebration of sport as inherently artistic, but even more the way in which beautiful movements on the playing field are etched forever in the memory and then again in talk. Like a good poem, each game can be read over and over again, with a multitude of different interpretations.

Declan Kiberd

CONTENTS

FOREWORD

by Tom Humphries

A long time ago during the time of innocence which was the 1990 World Cup Finals, a friend of mine, a man of Kerry, fell into a bout of wildly patriotic and foolish wagering on soccer, a sport about which he had a sketchy knowledge but a welling enthusiasm.

The tournament finished and, like many who had actually travelled to the event, my friend found himself with a large debt to hump around between his shoulders. Being a man of honour who valued his kneecaps, he took on extra work in the evenings and for a short while he was employed as a wine waiter in a well-known restaurant in Killarney.

The initial stages of his employment went well, it still being the tourist season and tourists being happy, charmed even, to be presented with a sommelier who was a little frayed around the edges. When things got quieter in the autumn, however, a problem arose between my man and the local clientele.

The restaurant might be entertaining, say, a local rotarian out with his family, a local business suit hustling for business, or a blade out for the evening and seeking to impress his latest squeeze, and my man would, when called upon, present the wine list and stand back, head tilted.

A bottle from the upper altitudes of the price range might be selected and fetched while all the time my man would smile and smirk politely as an accompaniment to his attentive bows and clicking heels.

The bottle would be fetched, brought to the table and presented in the correct manner before being opened and a small tincture poured into a glass for the customer to taste and offer his learned opinion on.

It was at this point in the ritual that my friend found it impossible to maintain the demeanour of reverence and respect so necessary for a man in his position. The customer might swirl his wine in his glass, give it a knowing little sniff and then sip the nectar slowly and judiciously letting it settle on the palate as my friend all the while inspected the ceiling in a posture of conspicuous indifference. Finally the tasting done, the table looking anxiously on, the customer would turn to my friend and say, 'that's excellent thank you'.

At which point my friend would nod solicitously and mutter slowly but audibly before commencing the pouring, 'like you'd effing know'.

As a Dub and as a newspaper sportswriter (a vocation for those good at neither sports nor writing it is said) I find myself in a similar position to the unfortunate customer when asked to consider a book of poetry by a Kerryman, a book which addresses the sacred matter of football. No matter how earnestly I commend and preface the following pages there will be those who will say, 'like you'd effing know'.

I know this though, I know that these poems touch the heart of what is important in our culture. I am sure *Beowulf* was good crack in its own time and that *Caoineadh Airt Uí Laoghaire* is every bit as much fun as the title suggests, that Robert Southey's *Roderick, The Last of the Goths* does indeed contain the basis for a very good sitcom, but none of them touch the day-to-day lives of the community. So little poetry deals with the topics that course through our daily conversation, the real names that stilled our childish play.

I had a beloved teacher in school, Brendan Leahy, a Kerryman of Knocknagoshel and a brilliant coach, who in his efforts to inspire me once told me a story of asking an old man at home in Kerry what football meant, what an All-Ireland medal meant. I wish I could remember the old man's name (I'd guess it was Eddie Walsh), but the story came to me many years ago. Anyway after a while the old man replied, 'Listen, I have five All-Ireland medals. So and so down the road, he has four.' Then he added with a modest laugh, 'I'd say there's a lot more thought of me now than there is of him.'

It was meant half in jest, but the point was there. Football is as good a measure of a man as so many of the things which poets concern themselves with. And in Kerry football is unique as a cultural force. I love when I am in Tralee, say, to stand at that point where you can see the places of business of Charlie Nelligan, Bomber Liston, Mikey Sheehy, Darragh Ó Sé, Seanie Walsh and Micko's chipper. I love to see how, almost involuntarily, people will glance through the windows of the auctioneers or the bakers just to see if one of the gods is in residence within.

Footballers in Kerry have a standing which speaks to us of the game they play. Every place name rings out with the names of its own heroes. Currow. Templenoe. Gneeveguilla. Ventry. Sneem. Valentia. Waterville. Dromid. Finuge. On and on. Places that have no meaning without their footballers' names attached.

The landscape is altered by the presence of football, the sentinel nets behind the towering posts, the aprons of perfect green seized from the grudging, rock-acned earth, the random architecture of clubhouses and dressing-rooms. And lately floodlights. Modest stands. Artificial turf. As Jackie Lyne said: 'With those bastards of mountains in front of us and those hoors of lakes behind us, sure there is nothing to do but play football.'

The weather interferes with the land, the fish and the football. Mostly though with the football. Divisional championships played out against the weather in November and December. Training nights and lads leaving dressing-rooms when the grass crunches under studs with the hoar frost down since dusk and the great belching issue of steam from the showers still ninety minutes of pain away.

Football is past, present and future. Legends and lore. From the ghost train to Aeroplane O'Shea. From Gega to Roundy and Purty and Páidí. Jerome O'Shea's catch.

Mikey's goal. Danno's horseshoe. Connell's gloves. Galvin's black book. The Pony from Shronedraugh.

That Gabriel Fitzmaurice should have turned his lyric mind to the language and culture of his tribe is right and fitting. When Gabriel writes of the North Kerry final of 1983, the weather cold and bleak, of the cup going back to Moyvane, of the bonfires and the hoarseness and all the men who went out before and came home with losers' medals, you get a sense of the communal yearning, of Moyvane's five lost finals since their win in 1966, of a break from a hunger which has been elemental in its impact on lives.

Mikey Sheehy, that great gentleman of Tralee, is remembered differently. Everything about Mikey suggests lightness and movement and grace. I grew up on the wind-scarred terrace of Hill 16 watching Mikey's lithe genius undo my heroes so many times. He was and is the essence of what the game should be and Gabriel catches Mikey's glory perfectly.

The Bomber is a different sort of turret on the Kerry landscape. Mick Hennessy's legend was new to these eyes and ears, but set forever in the concrete of verse. The Munster Football Final of 1924 tells us all we need to know about football's place in Kerry lives.

Gabriel's poems unfold line by line like the games themselves. We never know where they will take us, what we will discover about ourselves before the end. The great players have a different way of seeing the world, a different understanding of time and space. The great writers have the same facility. A different understanding of the things we take for granted, a way of seeing the things we all see but differently, with more grace and acuity and angles.

Football itself is the poetry of life in Kerry. The laureates of the game have earned the tribute gathered here, they have their deeds and dances matched with words and paeans. The first page I opened, the first line hit me so hard I knew it would stay with me forever: 'Whatever way it's kicked out, face the ball!'

Words to live by. Words to play with. Words of celebration. All here.

Great things are not done by impulse, but by a series of small things brought together.

Van Gogh

The white heat of Croke Park has started to cool in the memory along with the evenings.

Time to take stock, recharge. Ask the annual question: is it worth it? The journey? I've never known life without football. From childhood, the Duí, the Sem, minors, Under-21s, 1975, four-in-a-row, captaincy, West Kerry, newspaper, sniping, bidding for the manager's job, getting the manager's job, Under-21s, training, meetings, interviews, seniors, selections, rows, All Irelands, celebrations. No stops. Endless grief.

Páidí Ó Sé

HENCE THE SONGS

i.m. Billy Cunningham, singer

How soon great deeds are abstract …

Hence the songs –
The mighty deeds the tribe sings in the bar:
Gaisce diminished by the video.

Men I never knew still star
In North Kerry Finals,
Their deeds not history but myth
Alive upon a singer's breath;

Again local men are martyred
In a lonely glen;

Now love is lost,
A Rose is won –

Things insufficient till they're sung …

gaisce: (Irish) valour, great exploits, boasting

Sean Óg Ó hAilpín ... His father's from Fermanagh, his mother's from Fiji – neither a hurling stronghold.

Mícheál Ó Muircheartaigh

The great fallacy is that the game is first and last about winning. It's nothing of the kind. The game is about glory. It's about doing things in style.

Danny Blanchflower

SINGING PADDY ENRIGHT

We still sing Paddy Enright's football songs
From the 'twenties and the 'thirties, from a time
When people knew their poets: they belonged,
They bound their tribe together in a rhyme.
Poetry today does not belong,
Poets don't sing a people in a rhyme;
For eighty years we're singing Enright's songs:
Who'll remember us in future times?
So what?, you say, *We have a greater theme*
Individual as the poet in his mind.
Yeah! But no one needs it, poets are deemed
Redundant as their verses are refined.
Give me a people's ballads any day,
The rougher road where I must make my way.

A number of times it has been reported that I am in favour of the introduction of professionalism into Gaelic football. True, I have mentioned it a few times and as a result have been accused of preaching a heresy. Before elaborating on my concept of professionalism at all let me quickly add that my motives for considering it are purely in the interest of improving the standard of the game. To provide a standard that would encourage youngsters to play the game and that would give spectators something worthwhile to see.

Mick O'Connell

THE VOICE: MÍCHEÁL O'HEHIR

What county did he come from? We never knew.

All we knew of him was in his voice;

Everything it told us, we took as true.

He was our Sunday; he was the people's choice,

Our inspiration in a humdrum place;

He raised men up to greatness with his words;

Pre TV, we never saw his face,

The voice of the young republic; but we heard.

A 'fifties stay-home-Sunday afternoon,

We gather 'round the radio for the match

As Ireland becomes a parish in such rooms …

No voice, but John McCormack's, was a patch

On the voice that brought us visions on the air

As we turned on, tuned in to Mícheál O'Hehir.

The Goal-Keeper, like the poet, is born, not made.

Dick Fitzgerald

A Kerry footballer with an inferiority complex is one who thinks he's just as good as everybody else.

John B. Keane

Teddy McCarthy to Mick McCarthy, no relation, Mick McCarthy back to Teddy McCarthy, still no relation ...

Mícheál Ó Muircheartaigh

UP DOWN!

Moyvane, Co. Kerry. September 1959. I was six years old and Kerry had just won the All-Ireland Senior Football Final. We were the greatest as we shouted 'Up Kerry!' the length and breadth of the village. The Kerry team weren't mortal – they were gods and they walked among us every day. We lived in our own story – the story of football which had its own mysteries, and today they were glorious. We had resurrected from defeat and ascended into heaven where we were crowned champions of all Ireland. We would live in that reflected glory all year.

It was 1960 and I had just turned seven. At seven you think that all things can be known. Growing in facts if not in knowledge, I regarded the world as a sure and certain place, a place of predictable outcomes, a world of black and white. In this world, Moyvane was the centre and Kerry were the greatest. It was 1960 and I'd never even heard of County Down.

Things were changing in the village in 1960. By then the village had 'the electric light'; our Yanks began to visit us from New York and New Orleans; and a new water scheme was begun. It was proposed to pump water from the River Gale below the village to a huge water tower which was being built in Collins' field up the Glin Road, which would supply the whole parish. Among the many things we learned that summer were new names. Now a caterpillar was no longer just a creepy-crawly that ate cabbage, it was a great big track machine; surnames we'd never heard of in our parish now came to work among us – names like Seán Treacy and especially Malachy McMullen.

Malachy McMullen drove the Caterpillar. He spoke in a funny accent. We were fascinated by it. We imitated his accent and we teased him because of it. He took it in great part. To us, he was simply not a Kerryman. Later we would know he hailed from County Down.

One Monday morning that summer, Malachy Mc-Mullen had a red and black flag flying on his Caterpillar. We children wondered what it was. It was the Down colours. They were playing Kerry in the All-Ireland Football Final.

Down? Where in the name of God was that? What sort of a name for a county was Down? How would you shout for them? 'Up Down?' Is that what you'd cheer? 'Up Down! Up Down!' we teased Malachy McMullen as we passed.

There were no televisions in Moyvane in 1960. Only radios. The streets were abandoned to the stray dogs as the whole village tuned into Radio Éireann for the match broadcast. Such names on the Down team as we'd never heard before – Eamonn McKay, Kevin Mussen, Tony Hadden were all strange music to our southern ears. The strange music won that day. Our gods were overthrown.

Even now I can remember facing Malachy McMullen the following morning. It wasn't so much that Down had won, as that Kerry were beaten. Beaten! We had no answer to the strange music. The following year, that music won again.

By then we knew that the world was not sure and certain, that things weren't black and white. It was a valuable lesson, one of the many we learned from football. There would be more lessons to learn, but I'll never forget the summer when our gods were overthrown – the first step taken on the way of the unknown.

AT THE BALL GAME

for Seamus Heaney

Everything out there you see
Is a version of reality
As heroes triumph over doubt
And bring their kind of truth about.

Each, according to his way,
Engages on the field of play,
And, urging on, the faithful crowd
Are cheering, praising, cursing loud
For beauty only will suffice,
Beauty to infuse our lives:
No cup, no trophy will redeem
Victory by ignoble means.

And, so, we take the field today
To find ourselves in how we play,
Out there on the field to be

Ourselves, a team, where all can see;
For nothing is, but is revealed
And tested on the football field.

The real glory is being knocked to your knees and then coming back. That's real glory. That's the essence of it.

Vince Lombardi

They had the hurling and they had the heart. But why wouldn't they, it's bred into them with their mother's milk!

Phil 'Fan' Larkin on hurling heritage

WHAT WE REMEMBER

Who refereed the Final in 'sixty-one?
No one can remember; when I ask
The village players (it was they who won),
No one can help me with my task.
Winners remember only victory,
It's losers who remember what is lost;
Winners are secure in history,
Losers can't forget, must count the cost.

Winners are secure in history,
It's losers who remember what went on,
Winners remember only victory,
Losers are the ones who must go on
With what it felt like on the field of play,
The referee who wronged them on the day.

Con Brosnan was the political Bridge Builder of our time. And remember it wasn't always popular to try breaking moulds in those days. But Con had incredible guts and, regardless of pressure from within his own side of the divide, or from our side, he did what he believed had to be done to bring about peace and healing. He was the ultimate peacemaker in Kerry football after the Civil War.

John Joe 'Purty' Landers

MUNSTER FOOTBALL FINAL
1924

Nothing polarises like a war,
And, of all wars, a civil war is worst;
It takes a century to heal the scars
And even then some names remain accursed.
The tragedies of Kerry, open wounds –
John Joe Sheehy on the run in 'twenty-four,
The Munster Final in the Gaelic Grounds:
There's something more important here than war.
John Joe Sheehy, centre forward, Republican,
Con Brosnan, Free State captain, centrefield;
For what they love, they both put down the gun –
On Con's safe conduct, Sheehy takes the field.
In an hour the Kerry team will win.
Sheehy will vanish, on Brosnan's bond, again.

You can't win derbies with donkeys.

Babs Keating before Tipperary played Cork in 1990

'It mightn't have been the prettiest goal,' commented Tyrone manager Mickey Harte, 'but it was pretty effective today.'

Quoted in the Irish Times, *16 March 2009*

Keep your eye on the ball, even when it's in the referee's pocket.

Christy Ring's advice to aspiring hurlers

A SMALL BOY AND HIS HERO

Just a small boy gaping at his hero,
He's been this man so often in his games,
He touches him with a torn piece of paper,
His hero turns and, smiling, signs his name.

... the memories, the fervour, the excitement, the passion, the unique atmosphere, the friendliness and welcome of the people, the tremendous joy on the faces of young and old when exemplary referee Paddy Russell from Tipperary sounded the final whistle. You can have your Croke Park, your corporate boxes, glitzy All Star awards, your high-tech media centres, centrally heated dressing-rooms and all the other modern trappings, but for me anyway, win lose or draw, a bad November day in Quilty, ham sandwiches, friendly faces, side-line tensions, meeting the quintessential grass roots club chairman such as T.J. O'Laughlin, local girl singing the national anthem in flogging rain, beats the lot. Long live the small rural club, long live the real grass roots of the association, long live the unpaid worker of the GAA, truly the heart and soul of Irish life and culture.

'Weeshie's Week', The Kingdom 2004

HEROES

Maybe there are no heroes –
Just people that we cheer
In our need for glory
Born of our fear

And the heroes we are cheering
Are much the same as we
As fear of being nothing
Is changed to poetry.

The legacy of heroes is the memory of a great name and the inheritance of a great example.

Benjamin Disraeli

I missed [the] '84 [All-Ireland Final] because of the knee. I'd worn it out. The doctor said it had more potholes than the road to Knocknagoshel.

Mikey Sheehy

I love Cork so much that if I caught one of their hurlers in bed with my missus, I'd tiptoe downstairs and make him a cup of tea.

Joe Lynch, actor

THE TEAM OF 'SIXTY-TWO

i.m. Garry McMahon

No logo here on jersey, togs or boot,
A team who played for pure love of a game
That reveals its players in their truth,
A team that asked no money, handled fame.
We got a lift to the wonder of TV,
To a distant village, a small set in the Hall,
We paid like all the others just to see
Our team's ascent to glory raise us all.
For we believed in heroes 'way back then
Who raised themselves to immortality;
Before me in that photo, fifteen men
Who from my youth were more than men to me.
That picture hangs where once a saint or pope
Would look down from the wall in pious hope.

TREAD SOFTLY ON MY DREAMS

All-Ireland Final Sunday, 1962. A very different Ireland to today. An Ireland without computers, Playstations or private cars. An Ireland that was waking up to the wonder of television.

There was no television in Moyvane in September 1962. Most people had no car. The creamery manager, Paddy Sugrue, our next-door neighbour, had. We were all football mad. We'd tune in to Radio Éireann and live the football match, catch by catch, kick by kick, score by score, to the voice of Mícheál O'Hehir. We'd do it again today as Kerry togged out against Roscommon in Croke Park.

Croke Park! The very sound of it was magic to our ears. Croke Park was a kind of heaven where men became colossi and mortals became gods in the mystery of Gaelic football. Even today, at a remove of over forty years, I can line out that Kerry team: Johnny Culloty, Seamus Murphy, Niall Sheehy, Tim 'Tiger' Lyons, Seán Óg Sheehy, Noel Lucey, Mick O'Dwyer, Mick O'Connell, Jimmy Lucey,

Dan McAuliffe, Timmie O'Sullivan, Gerry O'Riordan, Garry McMahon, Tom Long, Paudie Sheehy. That team photograph, published with the players' autographs *as Gaeilge* in the *Irish Independent* after the All-Ireland and sold as a souvenir subsequently, hangs on the wall of my study. I bought it in Margaret Walsh's newsagents in Moyvane shortly after the All-Ireland and kept it at home until I married and moved out. My father had it mounted and hung it up in his utility room. He gave it to my son John a few years before he died and I asked John to give it to me last year.

The reason I wanted it for myself again was that I was writing a sonnet about football, what it meant to us at that time, and what it still means to some of us today. The team of 1962 weren't in it for the money. 'One for the money, two for the show' goes Carl Perkins' song. Well, whatever about the show, those men weren't playing football for money. They loved the game, as we did; they believed in the game, as we did. Beaten finalists in 1960 and again beaten – and again by Down – in the semifinal in 1961, a victorious Joe Lennon proclaimed that Kerry football was years out of date. Well, it wasn't! Nor is it today.

In the sonnet, I tried to convey something of that day in September 1962. As I said, most people in the village had no motor car. There was no television in the village. Paddy Sugrue found out that an enterprising curate in Shanagolden in west Limerick had a television set installed in the local parish hall and that you could pay to see the game there. (This was a time between the sale of indulgences and the advent of bingo, and the poor man had hit on a sure-fire way of making a few bob for his parish.) Paddy Sugrue loaded his family and myself into his car and drove us to Shanagolden. The hall was packed – west Limerick people are as football-passionate as any Kerry folk. We gazed as the wonder of television grew in our hearts and minds. The ball was thrown in, the game was on. Garry McMahon scored the fastest goal ever scored in an All-Ireland Football Final. When the final whistle blew, Kerry had won the game by one goal and twelve points to one goal and six. The game, the historians tell us, wasn't up to much. A contemporary account (John D. Hickey's) describes it as 'as long as a month of wet Sundays; the most undistinguished, cheerless, unexciting and insipid All-Ireland Final ever played'. But to a child watching his first All-Ireland Final, and watching the newly introduced television at the same time, this was the stuff of dreams. And it's dreams, not facts, that sustain us. To this day, I can recall that hall, that crowd, that television, that match, that victory. I know there will be small boys and girls (I was nine years old in September 1962) who will be watching such finals in the years to come. I hope they will be worthy of their dreams.

You can discover more about a person in an hour of play than in a year of conversation.

Plato

Pat Fox has it on his hurley and is motoring well now ... But here comes Joe Rabbitte hot on his tail ... I've seen it all now – a Rabbitte chasing a Fox around Croke Park!

Mícheál Ó Muircheartaigh

AUTOGRAPH

Big Liam Flaherty of Kerry,
The best centre back in the game
Played in our village last Sunday;
I asked him if he'd sign his name.

He told me that he'd be delighted,
But I had no paper or book
So I rolled up my sleeve and said 'Liam,
You can write on my arm here, look!'

He signed his name in blue biro,
My classmates all ask for a peek
And I roll up my sleeve and I show them –
Now I won't wash for a week!

A GIANT NEVER DIES

i.m. Michael Hennessy of Moyvane and Ballyduff

'I come from sweet Knockauling,
John Bradley is my name
And I'm the king of hurlers
For hurling is my game.'

So sang young John Bradley
As he dashed from the TV
His head full of hurling,
Great deeds and bravery

On that Sunday in September,
All-Ireland Hurling Day,
The All-Ireland Final over;
He dashed outside to play

With a hurling stick and rubber ball,
He hurled on his own –
He'd no brothers or no sisters
And so he played alone

Whack! against the gable
Then run and leap and catch
Re-playing the All-Ireland,
Making it his match.

And then, his mind-game over,
He ran in home to Dad
And they talked of hurling heroes
And the mighty games they played.

Dad told him of the exploits
Of Big Mick Hennessy
Who played football for Knockauling
And hurling for Ballylee;

And how once upon a Championship
He was called to play
In the local Football Final
And on that selfsame day

When the football match was over
He played for Ballylee
In the County Hurling Final
In the great Park of Tralee.

In the centre for Knockauling,
He scored five points that day
And when the match was over
He left the field of play,

No time to celebrate and lift
The cup of victory –
He dashed out to the hackney car
That would take him to Tralee
And changed Knockauling's colours
For the green of Ballylee.

Just in time for the second half,
His team a goal behind,
Big Mick Hennessy took the field
And hurled into the wind;

And when the game was over
He'd scored three goals to win
And thousands knew they'd never see
The likes of him again.

* * *

The time is some weeks later,
The place – the Park, Tralee,
The County Hurling Final,
Tullybeg and Ballylee.

John Bradley and his Daddy
Have travelled here this day,
A treat for young John's birthday –
Eleven years today.

The game is fast and factious,
And at half time they see
The men of forty years ago,
Knockane and Ballylee,

As thirty men in suits walk out,
The hurlers of that day
When Big Mick Hennessy showed to all
How the great can play;

And as his name is called out
Each man waves to the crowd
And at the name 'Mick Hennessy'
The cheers are long and loud.

But young John Bradley's puzzled –
The man he sees out there
Is not as he imagined:
With glasses, thinning hair,

To young John he looks no different
To the other men
Standing out there on the field.
He realises then

That Mick Hennessy's a story
Of a giant with a ball
And what he sees there on the field
Is not a giant at all.

Yes, Mick Hennessy's a story –
One that will be told
When Big Mick is dead and gone
And young John Bradley's old.

For a giant lives in story
Among his people who
Believe in deeds of greatness
And honour all that's true.

Yes, Mick Hennessy's our story,
A giant with a ball
Who once upon a Championship
Won glory for us all.

My name is Gerry McLoughlin. I used to be a rugby player. Some called me 'Locky', others 'Ginger'. No one called me a coward. You could say I had my moments. A long time ago I played for Munster against the All Blacks. One hundred thousand people say they were at Thomond Park that day. Ninety thousand of them are liars. They've been at it for more than twenty-five years. Imagine lying to your grandchildren about a rugby match. I know why they do it, though. What happened that day can never happen again.

Gerry McLoughlin

I don't think there's a part of me that's left without a bruise.

Keith Wood

MUNSTER VERSUS THE ALL BLACKS

Thomond Park 1978

The All Blacks came with their haka

(Munster's more beer and tobacca)

But out on the field

The Reds wouldn't yield

And they bate 'em 'way out past Athlacca.

MUNSTER VERSUS
THE ALL BLACKS

Thomond Park 2008

'Low lie the fields of Athenry',
We praise you, men of Munster, for your feat;
18-16 to the All Blacks, you played with honour,
Thomond Park salutes you. No defeat.

Meath make football a colourful game – you get all black and blue.

Cork fan 1988

One thing is absolutely crystal clear and that is Tyrone have had a far more gruelling road to the decider than Kerry, and their clashes in particular against Armagh will stand them in great stead; it is generally accepted that one hard championship game is worth twenty training sessions.

'Weeshie's Week', The Kingdom *2005*

FOR EAMON LLOYD

When Munster played the Tigers, Welford Road
Was the land of heart's desire for every fan;
Match tickets were more valuable than gold.
I travelled ticketless with my teenage son
Just to be there in Leicester on the day
With Munster men and women for the game –
To find a likely pub and watch the play
Was as much as we could hope for until Eamon
Lloyd with whom we stayed, a Tigers fan,
Gave my son his season ticket for the match,
What money couldn't buy, this kindest man
Gave John his heart's desire. Old friend, we watched
The game on television. And Munster won.
'Twas nothing to your kindness to my son.

UP FOR THE MATCH:
THE ALL-IRELAND SENIOR
FOOTBALL FINAL 1984

It was all over at 5 p.m. When Ambrose O'Donovan received the Sam Maguire cup on behalf of Kerry, the point was made: the game was clean, the hill was quiet, order prevailed. Even if the game was more dogged than inspired, it was, so far, a quiet day.

Jack O'Shea headed for the Outside Broadcasting Unit amid much jostling and hugging and kissing. The supporters evacuated Croke Park. It was 5.10 p.m.

A silent evacuation by All-Ireland standards, the Kerry supporters mostly smiling and remarking to one another: 'This was sweet', and undefeated Dublin supporters all streaming down towards North Frederick Street and Parnell Square.

It was 5.20 p.m. and the Kerry supporters had, as always, congregated outside the Belvedere and Barry's Hotels. Johnny Walsh of Ballylongford, a stalwart of many a Kerry victory in the 1940s, stood with his son Barry, himself a former Kerry player, and a group of friends on the footpath outside the Belvedere. I stood there, too, waiting for a friend.

Streams of blue-festooned Dublin supporters strode by, rightly proud of their team and county. There was occasional good-humoured banter between the Kerrymen and the Dubs: 'It's a long way back to Kerry,' they joked; and we: 'It's a longer way back for the Dubs.'

It was 5.30 p.m. and a battalion of young Dublin supporters sang their way down the street. By now the Belvedere was crowded with Kerry supporters, and the steps leading to the front door were crowded with Kerry men, women and youths, many of whom were waiting to rendezvous with more tardy companions. The singing battalion approached the Belvedere. One of the leading standard bearers spat at the Kerry supporters on the path. No one took much notice: this was just an isolated obscenity to be taken in the spirit of the day. Johnny Walsh and his group remained in conversation.

The singing stopped. The Dubs, armed with flags, faced the Kerry supporters. Silence. Silence. Then loudly: 'Ye filth, ye filth', chanted the Dublin mob.

'If we were Glasgow Rangers supporters, this would be war', quipped someone on the steps a little nervously. 'Ye filth, ye filth', the chant continued. The Kerry group held ranks.

No more banter: this was confrontation – 'Ye filth, ye filth', from the Dubs; 'Go home and take yere *batin*'', from the Kerry crowd.

One blue-clad supporter flew through the air and planted a drop kick, Kung Fu style, on one of the Kerry lads. When he landed, the two wrestled briefly. Bruce Lee was repelled. There was no retaliation.

'Ye filth, ye filth,' howled the fifty-strong blue contingent. The people on the steps began to withdraw into the Belvedere Hotel. In a matter of minutes all the Kerry supporters would have been inside. There would be no broken limbs or broken windows today. I was in the front row. The blue ranks broke. Blue flags became cudgels and rained upon our heads. We protected ourselves. We repulsed the attack. We did not retaliate.

The blues reformed. 'Come on, come on', they taunted us with Gary Glitter's song. We didn't. It was not cowardice. The Belvedere was full of Kerrymen and, when it comes to brawling, Kerrymen can give as good as they get. 'Come on, come on', the taunt continued. We didn't. There were half a dozen or so of us left on the steps. The man beside me was wearing the Kerry colours – a green and gold cap. The only emblem that any of us left on the steps was wearing. 'Come on, come on.' We shook our heads. There were no more blows.

By now the management of the Belvedere Hotel was aware of what was happening. A porter came to the door and requested that the man with the green and gold cap either remove it or leave the steps. He ordered us all indoors. We stood on the steps facing Barry's Hotel.

Inexplicably, the blue battalion moved on. There was a sound of breaking glass as they smashed the windows of a parked car. A few gardaí arrived – too few, too late. It was 5.36 p.m.

I didn't know whether to laugh or to cry when I read Gabriel's poem about me. I ended up laughing. It was a great honour all the same.

Mick Galwey

MICK GALWEY: LOCAL HERO, INTERNATIONAL STAR

He was a county minor,
Played midfield but was slow,
Won an All-Ireland medal
But was smart enough to know

He'd not make it playing Gaelic
So he switched to rugby and
Became an international hero
Playing for Ireland.

Playing Gaelic football's
Not too lucrative,
The rugby network
Had more to give,
Now instead of commercial travelling
He's an executive.

At the famous playwright's funeral
The papers all were there
Noting the famous faces;
They noted this great player,

And in the queue I overheard
An old GAA man say
'If he was a small bit faster,
He'd be a poor man today.'

JIMMY DEENIHAN

Tough as honeysuckle
And hard as diamonds are,
Defender of our values
From every brilliant star

Who sparkles for a moment
Then disappears from view,
You hold the line at corner back.
Our one true north are you.

Jimmy Deenihan was tough. He'd always keep himself on the near side. He wouldn't hold on to the jersey – he'd hold on to the skin. You'd be got for holding on to a fellow's jersey. You couldn't be got for holding on to a fella's skin.

Charlie Nelligan

Champions aren't made in gyms. Champions are made from something they have deep inside them – a desire, a dream, a vision.

Muhammad Ali

SEÁN CAVANAGH

Money couldn't tempt you,
You played for love alone
For what you sought could not be bought
But won, and for your own.

Money couldn't tempt you,
The contract torn up
Made you, a true knight, worthy
For the raising of the cup.

Money couldn't tempt you,
You'd do battle for your own,
You raised it up, your Grail, your cup,
And brought it in glory home.

The men of Ireland were hurling when the gods of Greece were young.

P.J. Devlin (c.1924)

Ollie Murphy is after throwing so many dummies, you wouldn't see the likes in a creche.

Kevin Mallon on LM/FM local radio

The difference between winning a club and a county All-Ireland is when you get a slap on the back after the match, you actually know the person when you turn around.

Thomas Meehan of Caltra

JOHN QUANE

He could have played with better
But he chose his own;
Playing with his county
He'd never carry home

The trophy all aspire to
But that's not why he played:
If he played with another county
He'd feel he had betrayed

Himself, his art, his people,
So he plays out his career
Away from the glare of headlines.
And yet sometimes you'll hear

From followers of football
The mention of his name.
It's enough that they believe in him,
His way, his truth, his game.

I was a lazy fella and Dwyer made it his business to get me in shape. Down in Waterville he was like a father to me. Nothing would do him but to be out at something and he'd always rope me into coming along. Every day it was the same. Golf, badminton, football, snooker, darts, cards. Everything you could think of. If we weren't doing something, he wasn't happy.

Eoin Liston

EOIN 'THE BOMBER' LISTON

Small men need their trophies
To boast to you and me.
Great men need no trophies.
Take Eoin Liston – he
Gave his seven All-Ireland medals
To be auctioned for charity.
Great men need no trophies.
They make history.

Defeat? You've got to toughen, specially when it's a bad one. All you can do is let go for a while, unwind. Bit like victory really. I mean, it's the same as it ever was. Treat the two imposters the same. Plough on, take the hit, stand over everything.

Páidí Ó Sé

PÁIDÍ Ó SÉ

I remember that first victory,
Munster Final Day,
The days of doubt were over,
We were singing 'Páidí Sé!

Páidí Sé! Páidí Sé!'
As we danced out on the field;
Páidí Sé was God that day
But even gods must yield

To the times when they, forsaken,
Are taken from the throne
And we can't look them in the eye
Because of what we've done.

And all forget, forget, forget
But I won't forget the day
You were crucified before us
For following the way,

Your vision of the beautiful
Before all who would destroy
The grace that we believed in
When, with all the others, I

Rejoiced, friend, in your triumph
As the crown was won your way
And the multitude was singing
Hosannas to Páidí Sé.

THE GAME OF YOUR LIFE

for Bernard O'Donoghue

Whatever way it's kicked out, face the ball!
While wingers await delivery in space,
Centrefield must rise above the maul
And safely field, taking thought to place
The ball of fortune with the chosen one
And will him on to make the greatest use
Of what he's given: the ball passed on,
He solos towards the goal as play ensues.
For now's the time when great men must redeem
The story of the game from death, defeat:
The game of life's the story of a team
Who cannot rest until their task's complete –
To raise the cup, the cup that cannot pass
And raise it up in glory for the mass.

The toughest match I ever heard off was the 1935 All-Ireland Semi-Final. After six minutes, the ball ricocheted off a post and went into the stand. The pulling continued relentlessly and it was twenty-two minutes before any of the players noticed the ball was missing.

Michael Smith

DANCING THROUGH: MIKEY SHEEHY

Nureyev with a football,

You solo to the goal

Where the swell of expectation

Spurts in vain –

O master of the ritual,

O flesh of tribal soul,

Let beauty be at last

Released from pain …

Now grace eludes its marker

Creating its own space

While grim defenders

Flounder in its wake;

And the ball you won from conflict

Yields to your embrace –

Goal beckons like a promise …

And you take.

[Matt] Connor's short senior inter-county career began against Meath in a National League game at Tullamore in March 1978 and came to a premature end as a result of a serious car accident on Christmas Day 1984. During that all too limited spell the Faithful county forward provided many talking points, as he enhanced match after match with his brilliance in general play and an amazing consistency in finding the target in spectacular fashion. It is no mean achievement for any footballer or hurler to top an annual scoring chart for all games in a single year. It is something special, however, when a player fills that position for five years in succession. Connor did just that between 1980 and 1984, and with flair and a finishing technique that ensured that he chalked up superb totals each year. This was at a time when the game was rich in exceptional forwards with the ability to notch up impressive individual match returns.

Seán Óg Ó Ceallacháin

MATT CONNOR

It's not about the winning
And it's not about the loss,
It's about what life throws at us,
How you face into your cross.

Matt Connor, we remember you,
The man you dared to be,
The one who with a football
Broke through to poetry;

And when, young body broken
And you could play no more,
'Twas life then, Matt, not football
That called on you to soar.

For many men are broken
But few men have the grace
To rise out of their brokenness
And bless the cross they face.

And rise you did, Matt Connor –
The cup that wouldn't pass,
You accepted it and raised it up,
A hero, for the mass.

I'm not giving away any secrets like that to Tipperary. If I had my way, I wouldn't even tell them the time of the throw-in.

Ger Loughnane

And it looks like there's a bit of a schemozzle in the parallellogram …

Mícheál O'Hehir

One chance is all you need.

Jesse Owens

There are two things in Ireland that would drive you to drink.
GAA referees would drive you to drink, and the price of drink
would drive you to drink.

Sligo fan after 2002 Connacht final

NORTH KERRY
CHAMPIONSHIP FINAL 1983

To everyone their native sport,
That right was dearly won,
And we believe in football
As we believe in song;
Oh! We'd follow it to Heaven
And we'd follow it to Hell
And we'd follow it to Limbo
If the pitch was playable.

So it was to Ballybunion
In the year of 'eighty-three,
The thirtieth of October,
The weather cold and bleak,
We went to cheer the Boro
For the North Kerry Championship
And everyone remembered
We last won in 'sixty-six.

Our opponents, Ballylongford,
I first must sing your praise,
You played the ball and not the man,
You were fearless in the fray;
But to everything its season,
Our time at last had come,
When Joe Langan blew that last long blast
The field was fought and won.

Now in Listowel upon my soul
They bitterly complain
The match was played not on their pitch –
You'd swear they owned the game!
But God! The cheers, the shouts, the tears,
Our bards could sing again
When our captain shook that blessed cup
And brought it to Moyvane.

The game is won, my song is sung,
The bonfires blaze on high,
As we drink the cup of victory

And hoarse with triumph cry,

Let us think of men who played to win

Who were always runners-up

And now stand back and make a path

And let 'em drink a sup!

Whenever a team loses, there's always a row at half time, but when they win, it's an inspirational speech.

John O'Mahony

We're taking this match awful seriously. We're training three times a week now, and some of the boys are off the beer since Tuesday.

Offaly hurler quote in the week before a Leinster hurling final vs Kilkenny

Meath players like to get their retaliation in first.

Cork fan 1988

Tradition won't play any games or score any points for you.

Dublin forward Alan Brogan on Dublin's chances of winning a Leinster title where the other three teams left were Kildare, Laois and Wexford

You must play boldly to win.

Arnold Palmer

To give yourself the best possible chance of playing to your potential, you must prepare for every eventuality. That means practice.

Seve Ballesteros

They have a forward line that couldn't punch holes in a paper bag.

Pat Spillane on a Cavan football team

Colin Corkery on the '45' lets go with the right boot. It's over the bar. This man shouldn't be playing football. He's made an almost Lazarus-like recovery from a heart condition. Lazarus was a great man but he couldn't kick points like Colin Corkery.

Mícheál Ó Muircheartaigh

ACKNOWLEDGEMENTS

Acknowledgements are due to Radio Kerry *(Terrace Talk)*, the *Terrace Talk Ireland* website and *The Kerryman* where several of these poems have been broadcast or published.

OTHER BOOKS
BY GABRIEL FITZMAURICE

Poetry in English

Rainsong (Beaver Row Press, 1984)

Road to the Horizon (Beaver Row Press, 1987)

Dancing Through (Beaver Row Press, 1990)

The Father's Part (Story Line Press, 1992)

The Space Between: New and Selected Poems 1984-1992 (Cló Iar-Chonnachta, 1993)

The Village Sings (Story Line Press; Cló Iar-Chonnachta; Peterloo Poets, 1996)

A Wrenboy's Carnival: Poems 1980-2000 (Wolfhound Press; Peterloo Poets 2000)

I and the Village (Marino Books, 2002)

The Boghole Boys (Marino Books, 2005)

Twenty One Sonnets (Salmon Poetry, 2007)

The Essential Gabriel Fitzmaurice (Mercier Press, 2008)

Poetry in Irish

Nocht (Coiscéim, 1989)

Ag Síobshiúl Chun An Rince (Coiscéim, 1995)

Giolla na nAmhrán: Dánta 1988-1998 (Coiscéim, 1998)

Children's Poetry in English

The Moving Stair (The Kerryman, 1989)

The Moving Stair (enlarged edition, Poolbeg Press, 1993)
But Dad! (Poolbeg Press, 1995)
Puppy and the Sausage (Poolbeg Press, 1998)
Dear Grandad (Poolbeg Press, 2001)
A Giant Never Dies (Poolbeg Press, 2002)
The Oopsy Kid (Poolbeg Press, 2003)
Don't Squash Fluffy (Poolbeg Press, 2004)
I'm Proud to be Me (Mercier Press, 2005)
Really Rotten Rhymes (Mercier Press, 2007)
GF Woz Ere (Mercier Press, 2009)

Children's Poetry in Irish

Nach Iontach Mar Atá (Cló Iar-Chonnachta, 1994)

Essays

Kerry on my Mind (Salmon Publishing, 1999)
Beat the Goatskin Till the Goat Cries (Mercier Press, 2006)

Translation

The Purge (A translation of *An Phurgóid* by Mícheál Ó hAirtnéide) (Beaver Row Press, 1989)
Poems I Wish I'd Written: Translations from the Irish (Cló Iar-Chonnachta, 1996)
The Rhino's Specs/Spéaclaí an tSrónbheannaigh: Selected Children's Poems of Gabriel Rosenstock (Mercier Press, 2002)
Poems from the Irish: Collected Translations (Marino Books, 2004)
Ventry Calling (Mercier Press, 2005)
House, Don't Fall On Me (Mercier Press, 2007)

Editor

The Flowering Tree/An Crann Faoi Bhláth with Declan Kiberd (contemporary poetry in Irish with verse translations) (Wolfhound Press, 1991)

Between the Hills and Sea: Songs and Ballads of Kerry (Oidhreacht, 1991)

Con Greaney: Traditional Singer (Oidhreacht, 1991)

Homecoming/An Bealach 'na Bhaile: selected poems of Cathal Ó Searcaigh (Cló Iar-Chonnachta, 1993)

Irish Poetry Now: Other Voices (Wolfhound Press, 1993)

Kerry Through Its Writers (New Island Books, 1993)

The Listowel Literary Phenomenon: North Kerry Writers – A Critical Introduction (Cló Iar-Chonnachta, 1994)

Rusty Nails and Astronauts: A Wolfhound Poetry Anthology with Robert Dunbar (Wolfhound Press, 1999)

'The Boro' and 'The Cross': The Parish of Moyvane-Knockanure with Áine Cronin and John Looney (The Moyvane–Knockanure Millennium Book Committee, 2000)

The Kerry Anthology (Marino Books, 2000)

'Come All Good Men and True': Essays from the John B. Keane Symposium (Mercier Press, 2004)

The World of Bryan MacMahon (Mercier Press, 2005)